NURSERY RHYMES

Mother Goose

MOTHER GOOSE RHYMES

Cuddly Critters

ANIMAL NURSERY RHYMES

compiled by Terry Pierce ∿ illustrated by Simone Abel

PICTURE WINDOW BOOKS
Minneapolis, Minnesota

Special thanks to our advisers for their expertise:

Terry Flaherty, Ph.D., Professor of English
Minnesota State University, Mankato

Susan Kesselring, M.A., Literacy Educator
Rosemount–Apple Valley–Eagan (Minnesota) School District

Editors: Christianne Jones and Dodie Marie Miller
Designer: Tracy Davies
Page Production: Angela Kilmer
Art Director: Nathan Gassman
The illustrations in this book were created digitally.

Editor's Note: Editorial and formatting decisions for most of the nursery rhymes in this book were based on the following source: *The Random House Book of Mother Goose* (1986), selected and illustrated by Arnold Lobel.

Picture Window Books
5115 Excelsior Boulevard
Suite 232
Minneapolis, MN 55416
877-845-8392
www.picturewindowbooks.com

Library of Congress Cataloging-in-Publication Data
Pierce, Terry.
Cuddly critters : animal nursery rhymes / compiled by Terry Pierce ; illustrated by Simone Abel.
p. cm. – (Mother Goose rhymes)
Summary: An illustrated collection of twenty nursery rhymes which feature animals.
ISBN-13: 978-1-4048-2344-0 (library binding)
ISBN-10: 1-4048-2344-1 (library binding)
ISBN-13: 978-1-4048-2350-1 (paperback)
ISBN-10: 1-4048-2350-6 (paperback)
1. Nursery rhymes. 2. Animals—Juvenile poetry.
3. Children's poetry. [1. Nursery rhymes. 2. Animals—Poetry.] I. Abel, Simone, ill. II. Mother Goose. Selections. III. Title. IV. Title: Animal nursery rhymes.
PZ8.3.P558643Cud 2006
398.8—dc22 [E]   2006027244

TABLE OF CONTENTS

Nursery Rhymes About Animals 5

Baa, Baa, Black Sheep 6

The Cat and the Fiddle 7

To Market 8

Three Blind Mice 9

Oh, Where, Oh, Where 10

This Little Pig 11

Mary's Canary 12

The Black Hen 14

Birds of a Feather 15

Cock-a-Doodle-Doo 17

Pussycat and Queen 18

Swan 19

Sing, Sing 20

The Robins 21

Bow-Wow 22

I Had a Little Hobby Horse 24

Gray Goose and Gander 25

Once I Saw a Little Bird 27

Fishes Swim in Water Clear 28

A Wise Old Owl 29

The History of Nursery Rhymes and Mother Goose 31

To Learn More 32

Index of First Lines 32

MOTHER GOO

NURSERY RHYMES ABOUT ANIMALS

If you like **DOGS** and **CATS** and **HOGS** and **RATS,** then you'll love these animal rhymes. Animal rhymes might have you **ROARING** with **laughter** or **PURRING** with joy. See if you can find a rhyme about your favorite animal.

BAA, BAA, BLACK SHEEP

Baa, baa, black sheep,
Have you any wool?
Yes, sir, yes, sir,
Three bags full,
One for the master,
One for the dame,
One for the little boy
Who lives in the lane.

THE CAT AND THE FIDDLE

Hey diddle, diddle,

The cat and the fiddle,

The cow jumped over the moon;

The little dog laughed

To see such sport,

And the dish ran away with the spoon.

TO MARKET

To market, to market, to buy a fat pig,

Home again, home again, jiggety-jig;

To market, to market, to buy a fat hog;

Home again, home again, jiggety-jog.

THREE BLIND MICE

Three blind mice, see how they run!

They all ran after the farmer's wife,

Who cut off their tails with a carving knife;

Did you ever see such a sight in your life

As three blind mice?

OH, WHERE, OH, WHERE

Oh, where, oh, where has my little dog gone?
Oh, where, oh, where can he be?
With his ears cut short and his tail cut long,
Oh, where, oh, where is he?

THIS LITTLE PIG

This little pig went to market,

This little pig stayed home,

This little pig had roast beef,

This little pig had none,

And this little pig cried Wee-wee-wee

All the way home.

MARY'S CANARY

Mary had a pretty bird,
    Feathers bright and yellow,
Slender legs, upon my word,
He was a pretty fellow.

The sweetest notes he always sang,
Which much delighted Mary;
    And near the cage she'd ever sit
To hear her own canary.

THE BLACK HEN

Hickety, pickety, my black hen,
She lays eggs for gentlemen;
Gentlemen come every day
To see what my black hen does lay;
Sometimes nine and sometimes ten,
Hickety, pickety, my black hen.

BIRDS OF A FEATHER

Birds of a feather will flock together,
And so will pigs and swine;
Rats and mice will have their choice,
And so will I have mine.

COCK-A-DOODLE-DOO

Cock-a-doodle-doo,
My dame has lost her shoe;
My master's lost his fiddling stick
And knows not what to do.

Cock-a-doodle-doo,
What is my dame to do?
Till master finds his fiddling stick,
She'll dance without her shoe.

Cock-a-doodle doo,
My dame has found her shoe,
And master's found his fiddling stick,
Sing doodle doodle doo.

Cock-a-doodle-doo,
My dame will dance with you
While master fiddles his fiddling stick
For dame and doodle doo.

PUSSYCAT AND QUEEN

Pussycat, pussycat, where have you been?
I've been to London to visit the queen.
Pussycat, pussycat, what did you do there?
I frightened a little mouse under her chair.

18

~ SWAN ~

Swan swam over the sea,
Swim, swan, swim!
Swan swam back again,
Well swum, swan!

SING, SING

Sing, sing,
What shall I sing?
Cat's run away
With the pudding string!

Do, do,
What shall I do?
The cat's run away
With the pudding, too!

THE ROBINS

A robin and a robin's son
Once went to town to buy a bun.
They couldn't decide on plum or plain,
And so they went back home again.

BOW-WOW

Bow-wow says the dog,
Mew, mew says the cat,
Grunt, grunt goes the hog,
And squeak goes the rat.

Whoo-oo says the owl,
Caw, caw says the crow,
Quack, quack says the duck,
And what cuckoos say, you know.

So with cuckoos and owls,
With rats and with dogs,
With ducks and with crows,
With cats and with hogs.

A fine song I have made,
To please you, my dear;
And if it's well-sung,
'Twill be charming to hear.

I HAD A LITTLE HOBBY HORSE

I had a little hobby horse
And it was dapple gray;
Its head was made of pea-straw,
Its tail was made of hay.

GRAY GOOSE AND GANDER

Gray goose and gander,

Waft your wings together

And carry

The good king's daughter

Over the one-strand river.

ONCE I SAW A LITTLE BIRD

Once I saw a little bird
Come hop, hop, hop,
And I cried, Little Bird,
Will you stop, stop, stop?

I was going to the window
To say, How do you do?
But he shook his little tail,
And far away he flew.

FISHES SWIM IN WATER CLEAR

Fishes swim in water clear,

Birds fly up into the air,

Serpents creep along the ground,

Boys and girls run round and round.

28

A WISE OLD OWL

A wise old owl sat in an oak.
The more he heard, the less he spoke;
The less he spoke, the more he heard.
Why aren't we all like that wise old bird?

THE HISTORY OF NURSERY RHYMES AND
MOTHER GOOSE

Nursery rhymes circulated orally for hundreds of years. In the 18th century, collectors wrote down the rhymes, printed them, and sold them to parents and other adults to help them remember the rhymes so they could share them with children.

Some of these collections were called "Mother Goose" collections. Nobody knows exactly who Mother Goose was (though there are plenty of myths about her), but she was probably a respected storyteller. Occasionally the rhymes commented on real people and events. The meaning of many of the rhymes has been lost, but the catchy rhythms remain.

Mother Goose nursery rhymes have evolved from many sources through time. From the 1600s until now, the appealing rhythms, rhymes, humor, and playfulness found in these verses, stories, and concepts contribute to what readers now know as Mother Goose nursery rhymes.

TO LEARN MORE

AT THE LIBRARY

Brauckmann-Towns, Krista. *Cat & the Fiddle and Other Animal Rhymes.* Lincolnwood, Ill.: Publications International, 1996.

Delcher, Eden. *Animal Rhymes.* Baltimore: Allan Publishers, 1992.

Wilkes, Angela. *Animal Nursery Rhymes.* New York: Dorling Kindersley, 1992.

ON THE WEB

FactHound offers a safe, fun way to find Web sites related to this book. All of the sites on FactHound have been researched by our staff.

1. Visit *www.facthound.com*
2. Type in this special code:
   1404823441
3. Click on the FETCH IT button.

Your trusty FactHound will fetch the best sites for you!

INDEX OF FIRST LINES

A robin and a robin's son, 21
A wise old owl sat in an oak, 29
Baa, baa, black sheep, 6
Birds of a feather will flock together, 15
Bow-wow says the dog, 22
Cock-a-doodle-doo, 17
Fishes swim in water clear, 28
Gray goose and gander, 25
Hey diddle, diddle, 7
Hickety, pickety, my black hen, 14
I had a little hobby horse, 24
Mary had a pretty bird, 13
Oh, where, oh, where has my little dog gone? 10
Once I saw a little bird, 27
Pussycat, pussycat, where have you been? 18
Sing, sing, 20
Swan swam over the sea, 19
This little pig went to market, 11
Three blind mice, see how they run! 9
To market, to market, to buy a fat pig, 8

～ LOOK FOR ALL OF THE BOOKS IN THE ～ MOTHER GOOSE RHYMES SERIES:

Counting Your Way: Number Nursery Rhymes
Cuddly Critters: Animal Nursery Rhymes
Forecasting Fun: Weather Nursery Rhymes
Friendly Faces: People Nursery Rhymes
Sleepytime: Bedtime Nursery Rhymes
Ticktock: Time Nursery Rhymes

Mother Goose

NURSERY RHYMES